In the crowded future

poems by

Greer Gurland

Finishing Line Press
Georgetown, Kentucky

In the crowded future

Copyright © 2021 by Greer Gurland
ISBN 978-1-64662-489-8 First Edition
All rights reserved under International and Pan-American Copyright Conventions. No part of this book may be reproduced in any manner whatsoever without written permission from the publisher, except in the case of brief quotations embodied in critical articles and reviews.

ACKNOWLEDGMENTS

I would like to thank Leah Maines, Christen Kincaid and the entire team at Finishing Line Press for their commitment to my work and their expertise.

Let me share how thankful I am to my husband, Ira, and our wonderful children Ian, Russell, Nathaniel, Sophie and Samuel for continuing to surprise me on a daily basis.

Publisher: Leah Huete de Maines
Editor: Christen Kincaid
Cover Art: Russell Gurland
Author Photo: Dave Rossi
Cover Design: Elizabeth Maines McCleavy

Order online: www.finishinglinepress.com
also available on amazon.com

Author inquiries and mail orders:
Finishing Line Press
PO Box 1626
Georgetown, Kentucky 40324
USA

Table of Contents

In the crowded future 1

March 29 2

Stay in the present 3

Someplace to park 4

"There is a cadence, she had been told, to the wind" 5

"The silver pots are stacked in threes" 6

So Much Beauty 7

"The sun knows nothing" 8

"Is it nicer outside on this summer day" 9

"Knobs on the dresser drawer" 10

"Not yet, sunset. Tonight, I am looking" 11

"Now that we can't just go out" 12

"I know the proportions are off in the collage I made in middle school" 13

"When I am gone do not rejoice too long" 14

"My soul is a squirrel" 15

"My sister and i shared a room" 16

"Sadness takes us backwards" 17

"Time by Love was one-timed wooed" 18

Worry 19

"And just now I see my neighbor" 20

"I will take a leaf over a flower any day" 21

"At the end of the world" 22

Fortune's Spindle 23

"Once in a while" 24

For all of you who help me, time and again, to see another way forward.

NOTE FROM THE AUTHOR

I wrote these poems during times that were very challenging for all of us who have had to cope with fear and uncertainty while trying to stay strong. For me, the process of writing these poems, in particular, has been life-affirming. They illustrate that no matter what we as human beings have to endure, we find a way to go on. We live in the small moments that have become so precious to me as I've grown older.

My hope is to connect with you, kind reader, if by chance a similar feeling about this precious and fragile life would have come to your attention. It is sharing that has always nurtured me and pleasantly surprised me when the thoughts are reflected back. I hope that you enjoy these poems which are simple and sometimes surprising but nothing outside of ordinary extraordinary life which we all share.

~G.G.

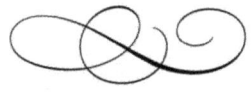

In the crowded future

What if they went ahead
with the old street fair
and the girl got lost again
not entirely accidentally.
Would I know whether
to scold her for sheltering
in place of holding my hand?
In the crowded future
when we see now alongside
the past, what will pale
what will recede like that
backwards branch
heavy with lonely birds?
Tonight, the night is a light.
Let's dream of the perfect
life: children all back
in school and you and I
busy and unaware.

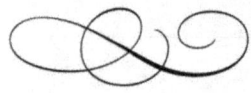

March 29

What is it that we hope to find
rising early under quarantine?
The birds have no idea why
so little competes with their song.
Maybe they notice the world
a bit quieter, a bit more intent on listening.
Only humans ask why
or choose not to ask to know more.
I can choose to think, or not to think
on the saddest things, though I am able to—
or so I thought. It seemed unthinkable, didn't it?
even when it started only half a world away.

Stay in the present

I do, but it is a funny kind of present
as if I am in the future looking back on now
savoring this jelly doughnut, holding this
view of my child's face in my mental hands.
No harm done, I suppose,
except that it tinges every joy with sorrow
or perhaps only sees the sorrow there
like the dusty ledge of a window
we must open anyway
for air. Strange habit, or flaw.
But no harm done,
I suppose. It started a long
long time ago
when I was still a child.

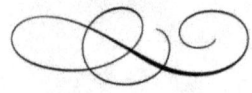

Someplace to park

I need someplace to park
where I can safely be
a witness to all nature
without it touching me.
The sun is too bright
for me to write, the cold
too much to bear, the birds
that swoop take too much
of me with them
and never land.
Find me a spot instead
to park
where I can safely be
the shady place
that overlooks the brook
that cannot speak.

There is a cadence, she had been told, to the wind. But stepping outside, there was no lullaby to touch the skin, only a faint smell of rain lingering on the petals of the spring blossoms about her feet. The air was crisp and the breeze fell patternless against her ribs.

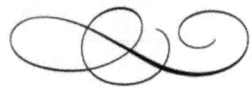

The silver pots are stacked in threes
and fives upon the linoleum floor.
The leaky sink I notice now
but then no more.
The cupboards are not bare
but overflowing, and the tin
for muffins
is clean, just upturned, its face to the floor.
Drip—there goes
knowing when and how to hear and see
and how to space out grief so that it looks—
almost—
like some other thing.

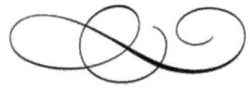

So Much Beauty

Sun after hard rain
like before the flood
of goodbyes.
What a strange time
for a bird call
as if nothing has changed
the bright white spring light,
the leaves like little flowers
on a tree branch
outside my window.
One car is far gone
by now.
I wished
for this silence
as a child: a day when life
and death were what we talked of
at the dinner table.
But not like this. Not like this.

The sun knows nothing
nor does it care
for the scarves about
our faces,
people dying everywhere.
What does the sun know?
What does the sun care?
Foolish thunder claps
then stops
and a rainbow appears.
The sun knows nothing still
nor does it care—
But you can tell by looking
that the blossoms know.

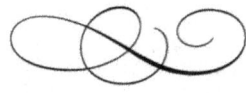

Is it nicer outside on this summer day
because I don't mind going.
No, the chairs are wet and it is cold,
too cold for a summer day
and yet it is
and so it is not too cold for a summer day
just not the summer day of my dreams:
Hot breeze begging me to stay, holding me
in place, upright like the spoon in a soup
bowl when it's good and thick,
the only way my grandfather would take it.

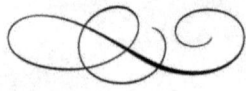

Knobs on the dresser drawer
invite the sun and shade
and play this afternoon
on the windowsill and floor
while a branch dances
beyond in a time that recalls
my childhood though the melody
eludes me still.

Not yet, sunset. Tonight, I am looking
at the leaves and branches that
nod like a sad head
over the quiet streets. No matter.
I don't see it.
I want something that is exciting as a perfect storm
but calm.

Now that we can't just go out
I miss doing the things
I never did:
going out on a whim
and taking myself to lunch
or shopping the afternoon away.
I miss simple things I gave away—
time in a crowded cafe
or a bookstore full of afternoon.

Small things, too—
that head massage,
or the rest for my wrists
in the salon with the special
price on a pedicure I'm sure
I still won't get once we are free
to make our own mistakes again
to choose to be solitary.

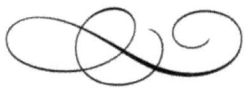

I know the proportions are off in the collage I made in middle school
that I just put up in my newly cleaned middle-aged room
but what is wrong with that jar I painted is recognizable to me—
and that comforts me.
I see what I did wrong, and I saw then.
So something is there. Something is the same.
Something is left of me.

When I am gone, do not rejoice too long
or linger while the nectar of a peach
slides down your chin and leaves unwanted streaks.
When I am gone, do not rejoice too long
while searching through a box closed far too long
and filled with recipes and photographs
lest you forget that you are not me at all—
though in your eyes and smile you will see
what I have known so wisely and so long:
that you are who I was meant to be.

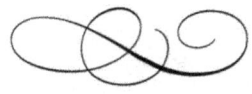

My soul is a squirrel.
I see it outside moving to a pause.
So still it stays, for some
nearby passing life
to see but not see, and be gone.
Now it stirs, busy again beside
a dandelion leaf,
digging up what might have been
a memorable place
had I not thought to look up.
Steadily, it seeks another place.

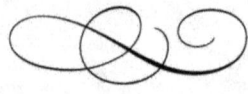

My sister and i shared a room
with two windows, a chest,
matching green bedspreads
and a strict divide—
her side, my side.
On the floor i played jax
until I got to ten and back,
or solitaire with an old deck until dark.
Then, above my twin bed I'd rest
my glasses which I kept close,
as close as I thought close gets.

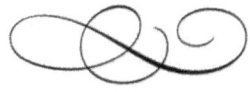

Sadness takes us backwards
and joy forwards in time.
A few steps back and stumbling on
is what we are meant to do.
For more time how much
would you endure?
The current takes the stream,
the babbling brook to the same
beginning-end
we marvel at all our lives. Here,
this is the spot where we knelt
and sent off paper boats we creased
quickly from scraps of the news
we never got to.

Time by Love was one-time wooed.
Time knocked on Love's wreathed door
To find Love busy doting on another
  paramour.
Time was too sick to speak, too ill
  was Time to carry on
'Till Grief held out its cane for Time
  to lean its weight upon.

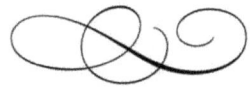

Worry

Set it off in the distance like
the hills that roll along.
Tac it to the clouds and let it fly
like seagulls on a silvery summer night.
Separate the feeling from the thought
like the egg white from the yolk.
But the perfect shell is hard, and night
does not fly with the gull.
The distance collapses,
and the mountains tumble, full
of the roots that took so long
to find a home. And the clouds
are never shapeless. We all know
they can appear to be almost
anything.

And just now I see my neighbor.
What he has been doing is dragging
new green pines to line
the fence that separates our yards.
He drags each tree and sets them two feet apart.
He might as well plant them crooked.
See mine, askew, forever in repose.
No, he will plant them straight as a tree,
tree of our imagination.
But who would think to plant
a tree crooked?
An overcast day. A good day
for planting.
I am happy for my neighbor.
Planting straight is easier.
I can see his hope.

I will take a leaf over a flower any day.
How common and unique,
how beautiful the leaf:
in a bold bunch, or as lone flag waving,
singing silently through my windowpane.
I could sit for hours in health or pain
admiring. But no one loves
the leaf like the tall or gnarled or wrinkled
trunk from which that green slip has sprung.
Behind each leaf, the axis silently
stands forever in the background,
bark covered. It must be more
than enough to see each leaf grow
and die and fall. Can it forget?
Or must the bole and bark look out
and see at once more leaves than any
human eye could?

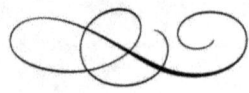

At the end of the world
a lonely man sits on a rock.
I am this man, holding all the love
in the world in my hand
where I have always kept it.
It is what has gotten me this far.

Fortune's Spindle

The morning was so warm
I asked the boy to walk the block
and name for me the nameless
common birds and trees
and small buds I can still
bend to see. And so we walked
that familiar way
but stopped to say: starling,
catchweed bedstraw
and the London plane.
Warm as moss phlox
afterwards I had to stay
outdoors and lie
while the lesser periwinkle
played about my feet. Once
a robin's red breast swooped
almost low as me, praying
but not alone—the basswood
making room for me—
I had so much company
which seemed a kindness to repay
and repay and why
from now on you'll see
me bend and whisper to the white
mouse-eared chickweed: *be still.*
I am Greer.

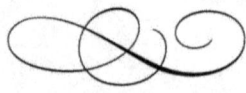

Once in a while
the sunlight seems to be full
of sorrow, like birds flying
not north or south but away
from what they cannot fly from.

Sunlight now, and I am writing
just so I can remind myself
I am not alone.

Greer Gurland is a student of Seamus Heaney and his influence shows. Ms. Gurland studied the craft of writing poetry with Professor Heaney at Harvard University. From Professor Heaney, she learned to use simple language to capture the complexities in our everyday. Ms. Gurland's short poems are not only for poets, per se. They are highly readable. They have also been described as deceptively simple. Ms. Gurland's poems resonate, revealing the extraordinary lurking just below the surface of the seemingly ordinary.

Ms. Gurland earned her degree in English and American Literature and Language from Harvard College in 1991. Ms. Lucie Brock-Broido selected her to receive the Academy of American Poets Prize for Harvard College. Ms. Gurland attended Harvard Law School, graduating in 1994. She then spent time raising a family and eventually advocating for children with special needs. During this journey, she discovered that writing remained an indispensable tool for forging meaning in the small moments that shape our lives, and for recording our humanity especially in times of uncertainty.

In 2017, Ms. Gurland won the Baumeister Creative Writing Scholarship from Fairleigh Dickinson University where she went on to earn her MFA in Poetry in 2020. Finishing Line Press published her debut collection *It Just So Happens…Poems to Read Aloud* in 2018. The volume won national acclaim including Human Relations Indie Book Award Director's Choice Award 2018 Life Experiences Book of the Year. *In the crowded future* is Ms. Gurland's second volume of poetry. Most recently, Ms. Gurland was chosen as a Finalist for the Moon City Poetry Award.

The poems in *In the crowded future* entice with their short forms and familiar, often conversational tone. In relatively few lines, they achieve a considerable depth and complexity. They frequently surprise or are wryly humorous. Ms. Gurland's themes suggest that she is a humanist in every sense of the word. By reading her work, one feels more human, at least more connected to the poet, and in a way that feels intimate, honest and ultimately, important.

www.ingramcontent.com/pod-product-compliance
Lightning Source LLC
LaVergne TN
LVHW041516070426
835507LV00012B/1609